Lots and Lots of Letter Tracing Practice!

by

Handwriting Time

Lots and Lots of Letter Tracing Practice!
by Handwriting Time

ISBN-13: 978-1512260526
ISBN-10: 1512260525

Part 1: Tracing letters

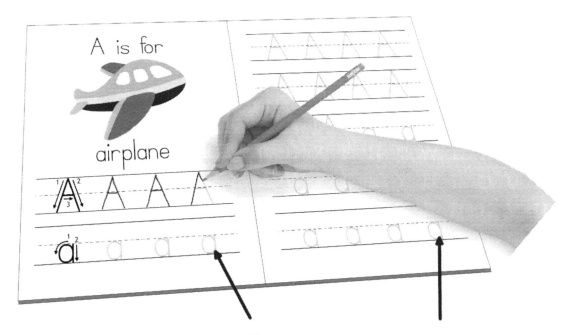

Follow the gray lines to
form the letters.

A is for

airplane

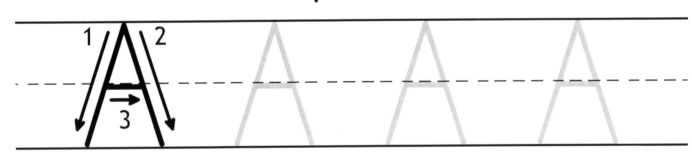

A A A A

A A A A

A A a a

a a a a

a a a a

B is for

bicycle

B B B B

B B B B

B B b b

b b b b

b b b b

C is for

cake

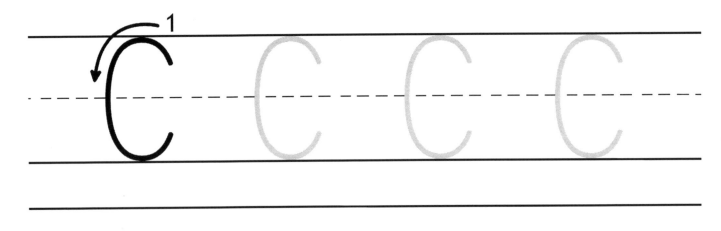

D is for

dinosaur

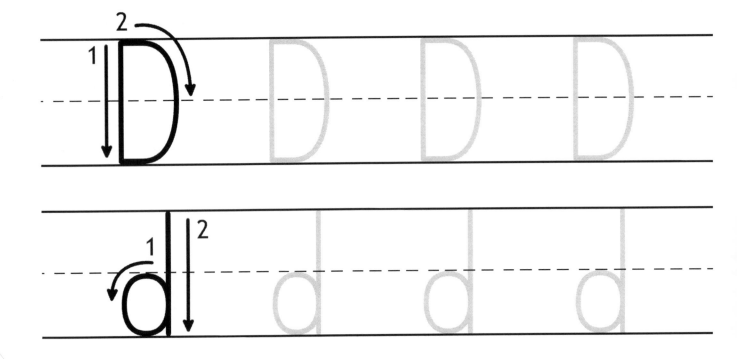

D D D D

D D D D

D D d d

d d d d

d d d d

E is for

elephant

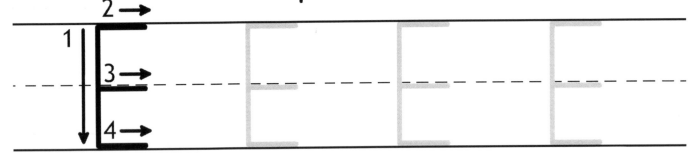

E E E E

E E E E

E E e e

e e e e

e e e e

F is for

flower

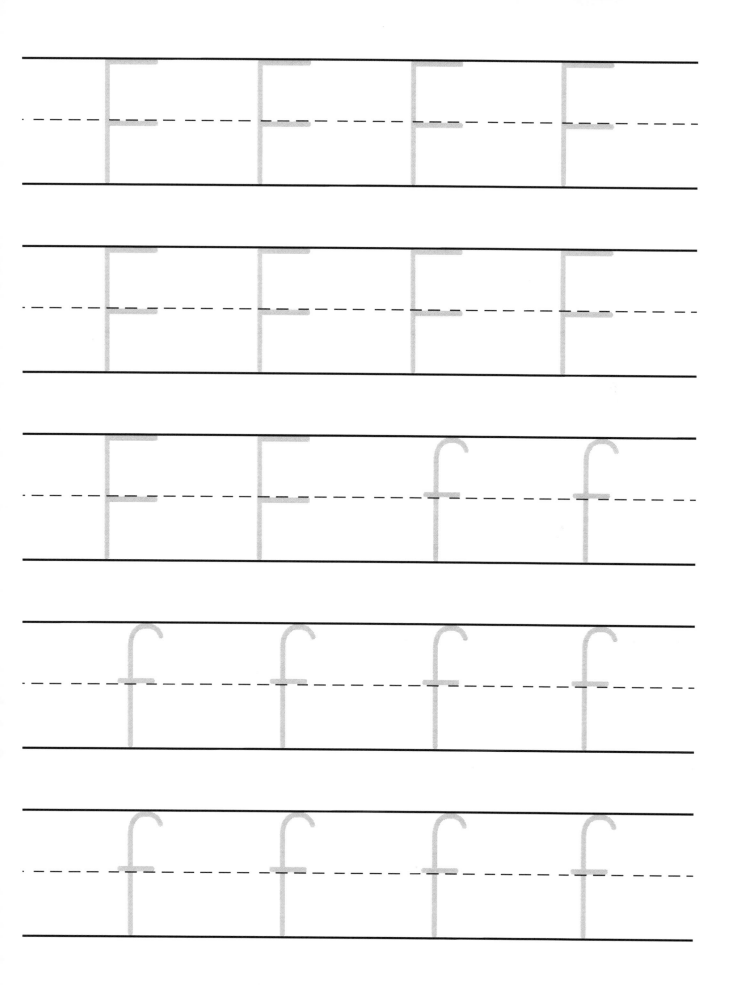

G is for

giraffe

G G G G

G G G G

G G g g

g g g g

g g g g

H is for

hedgehog

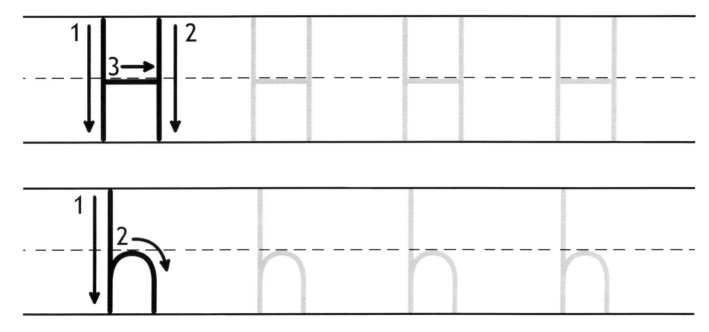

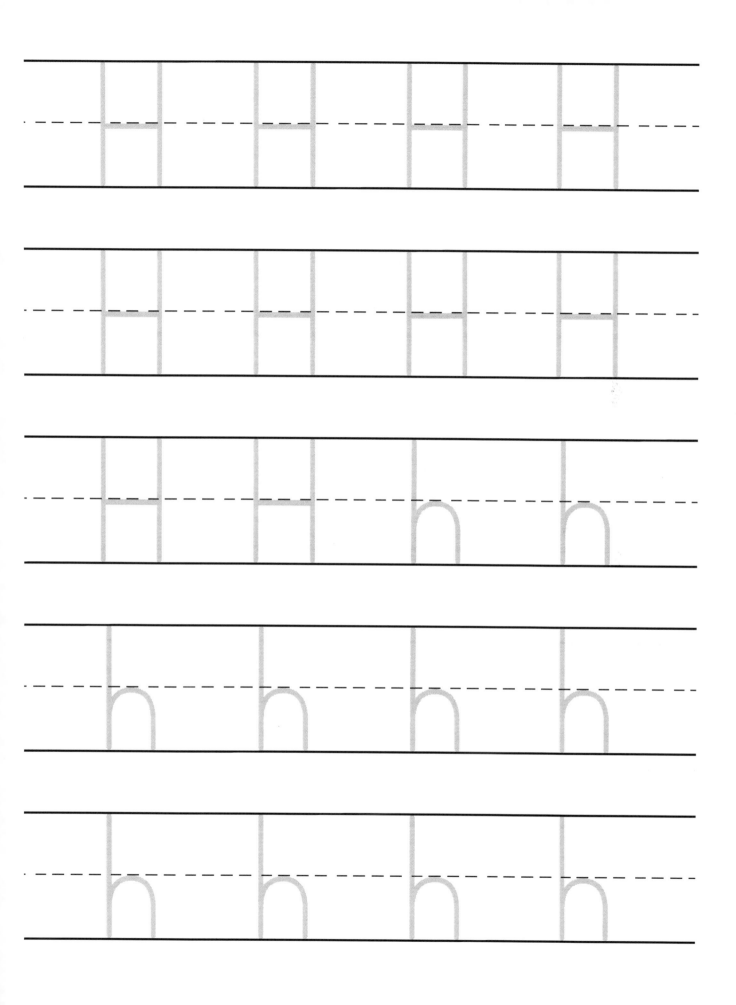

I is for

ice-cream

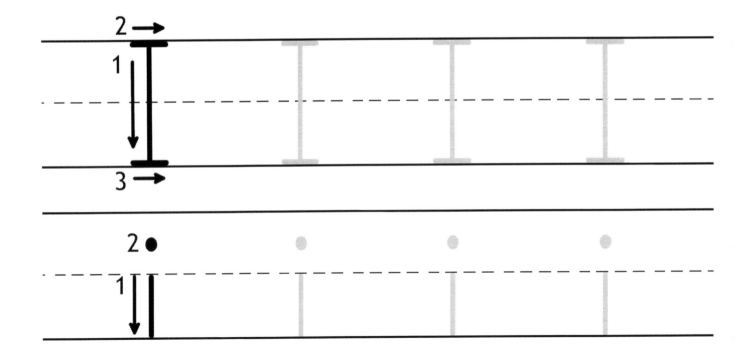

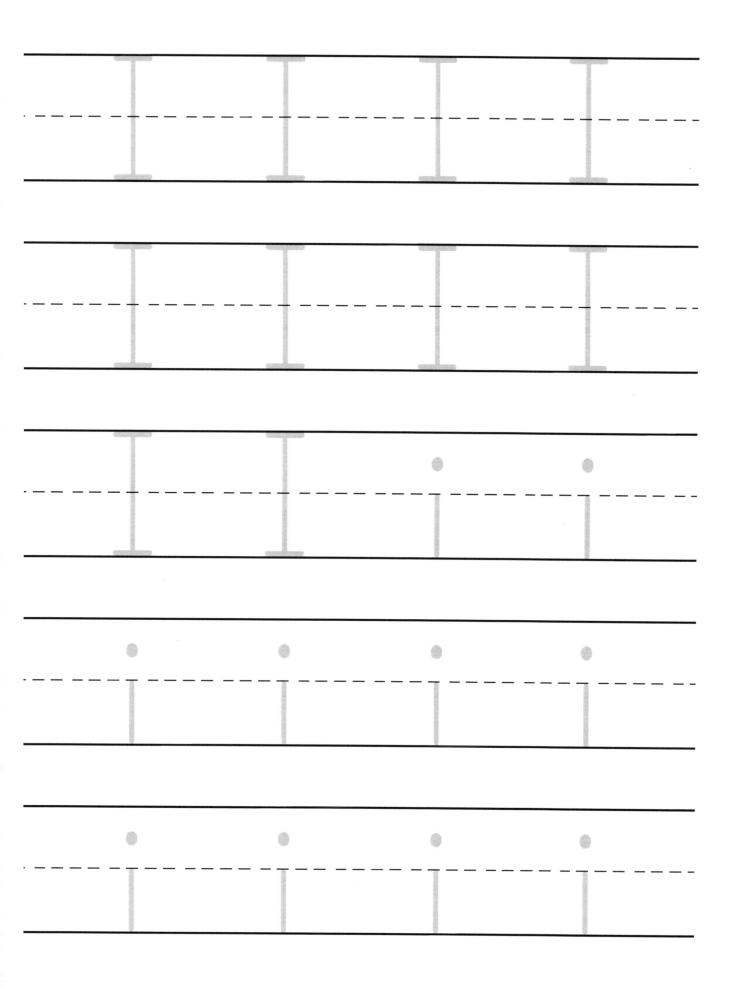

J is for

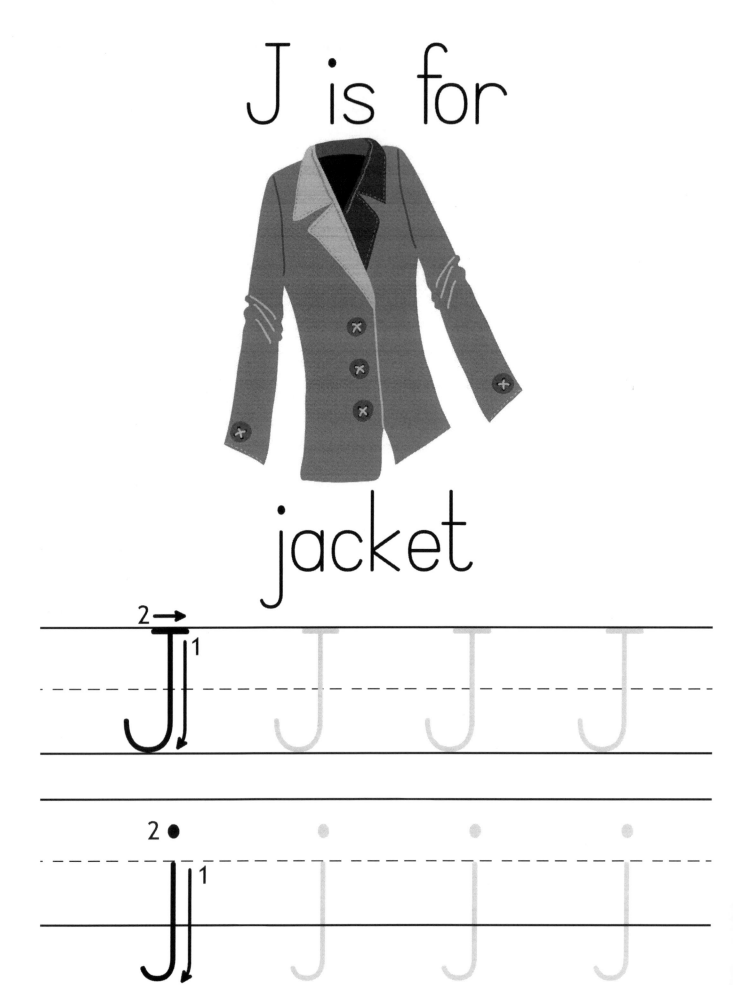

jacket

J J J J

J J J J

J J j j

j j j j

j j j j

K is for

kangaroo

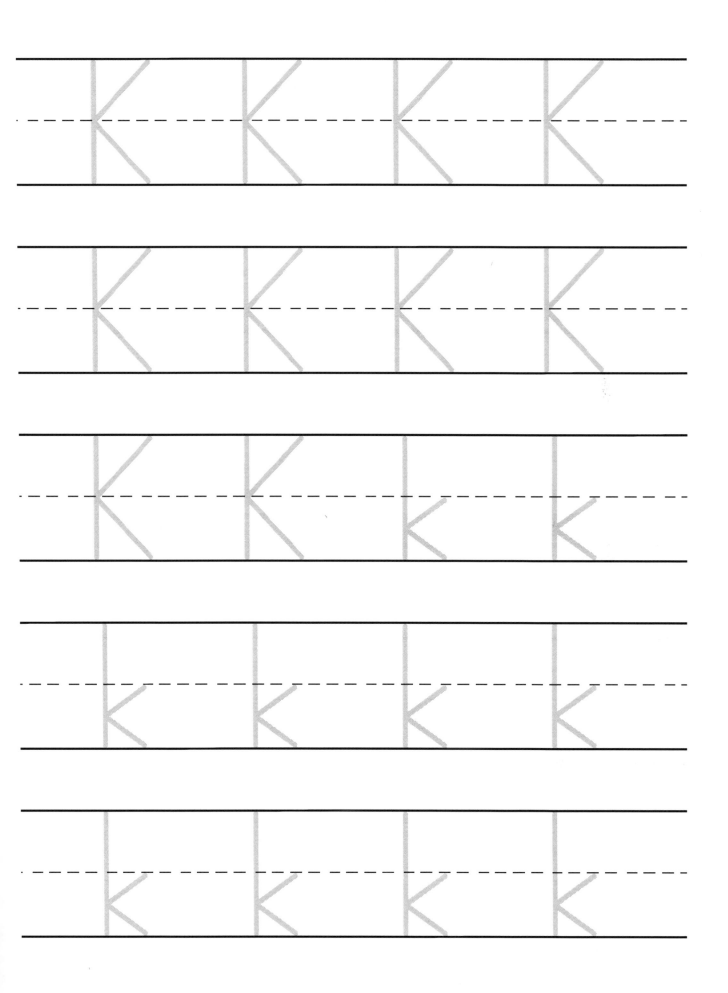

L is for

lion

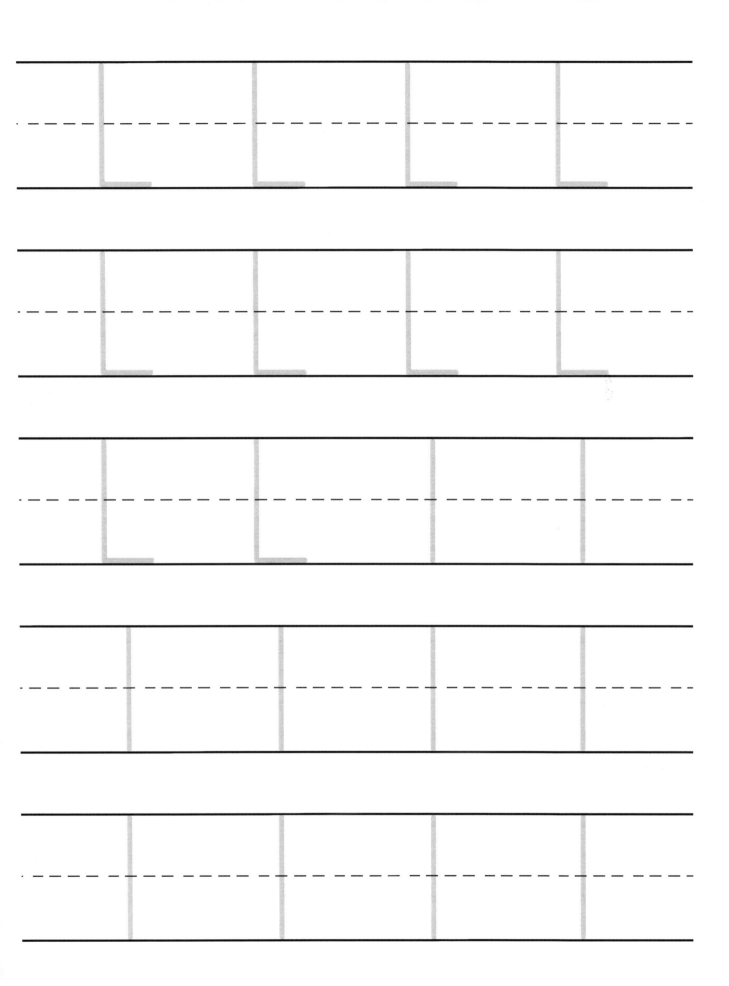

M is for

mushroom

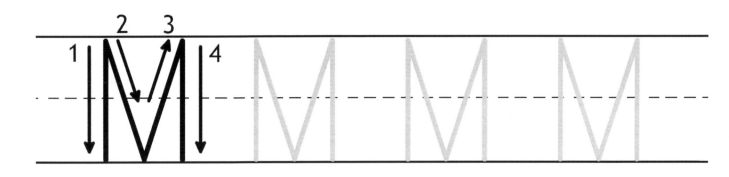

N is for

needle

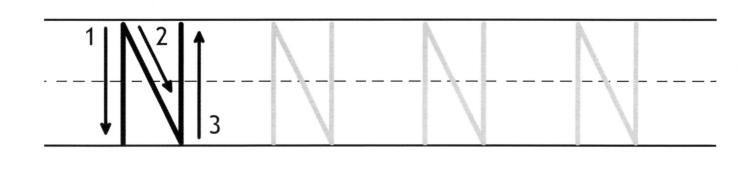

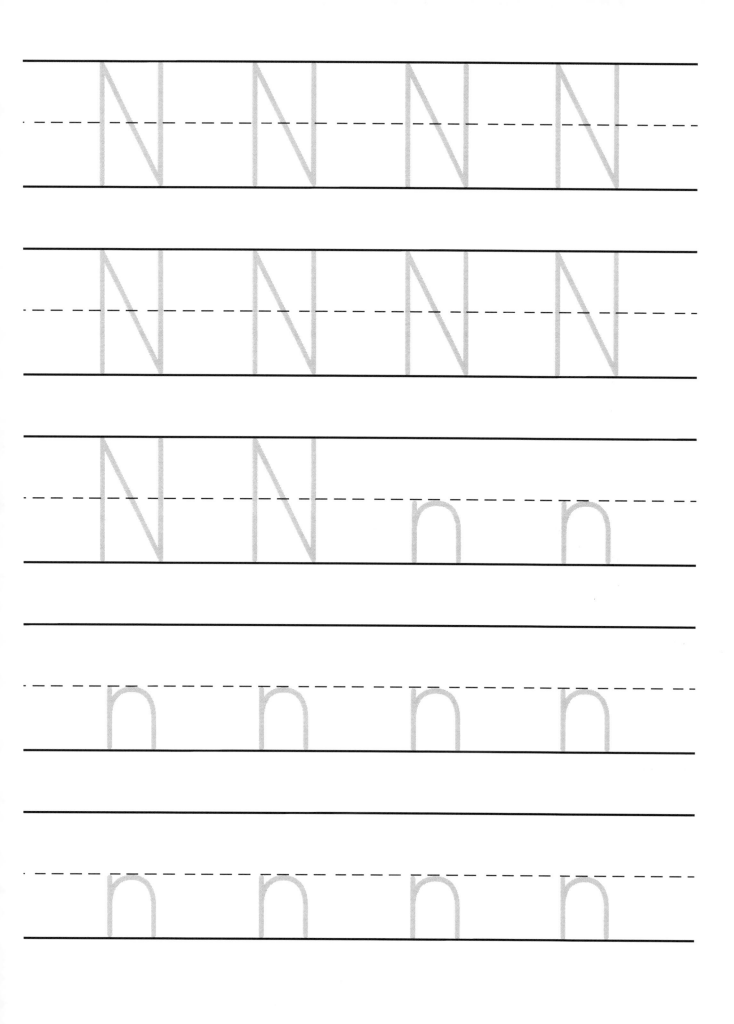

O is for

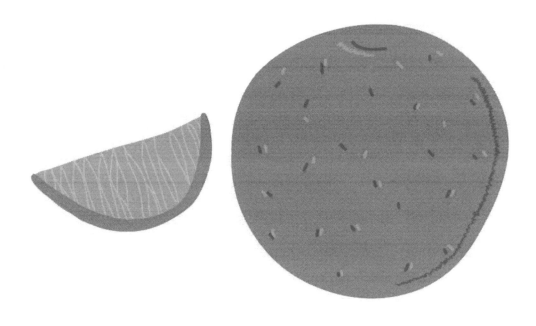

orange

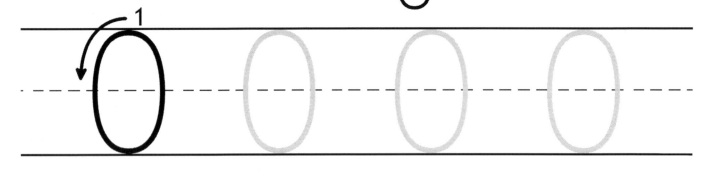

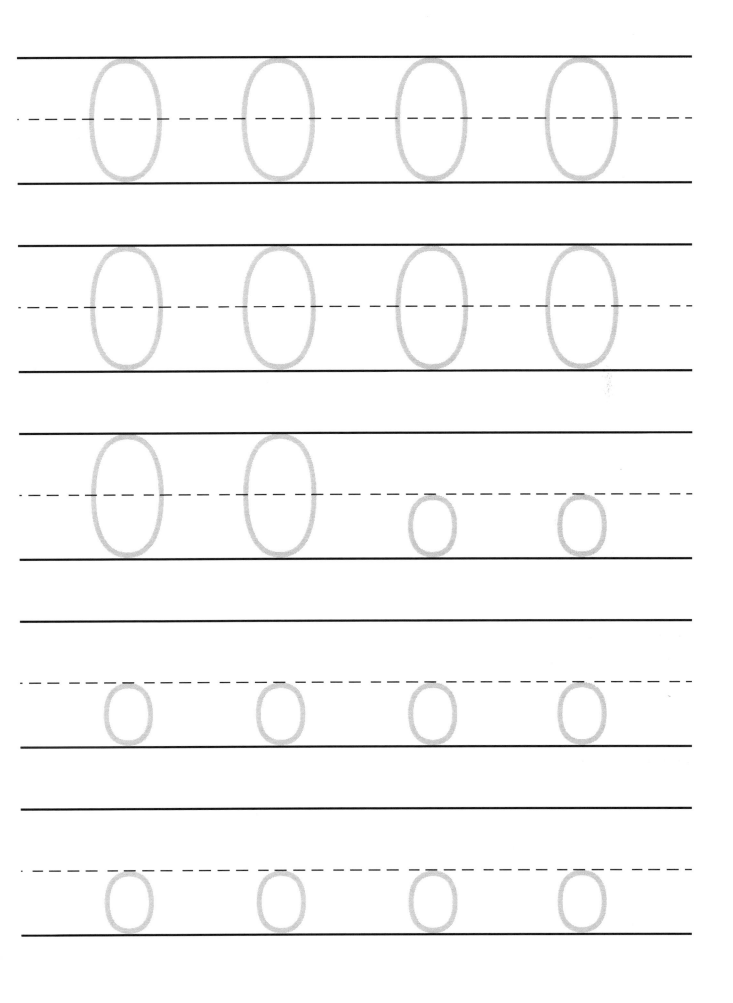

P is for

pineapple

P P P P P

p p p p p

P P P P

P P P P

P P p p

p p p p

p p p p

Q is for

queen

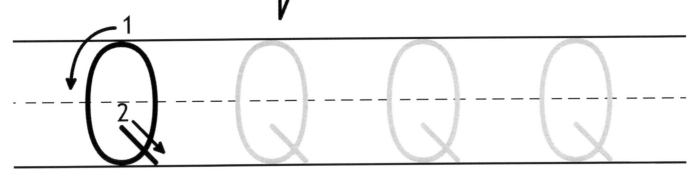

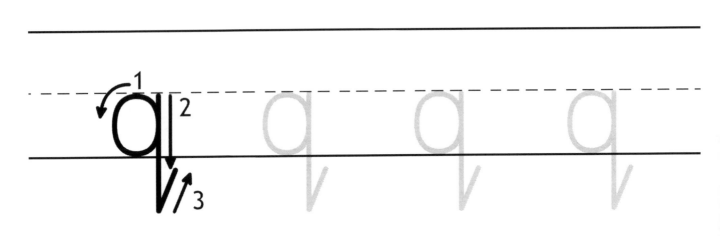

QQQQ

QQQQ

QQ q q

q q q q

q q q q

R is for

rainbow

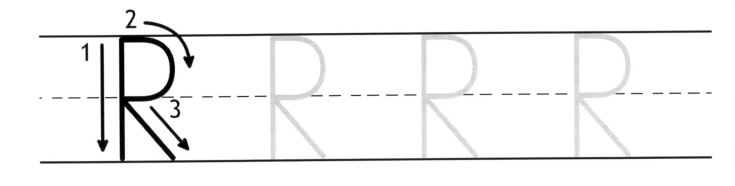

R R R R

R R R R

R R r r

r r r r

r r r r

S is for

scissors

S¹ S S S S

S¹ S S S

S S S S

S S S S

S S S S

S S S S

S S S S

T is for

tortoise

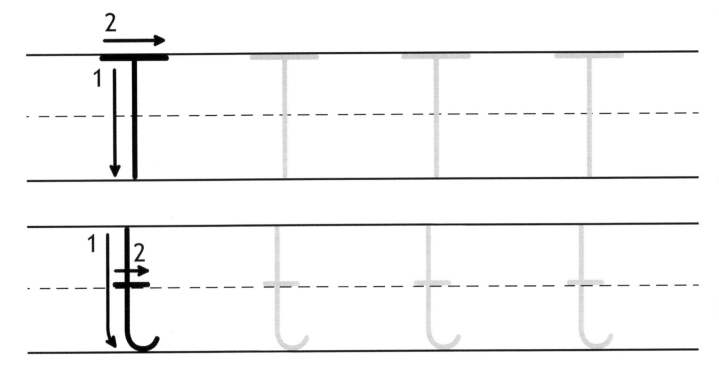

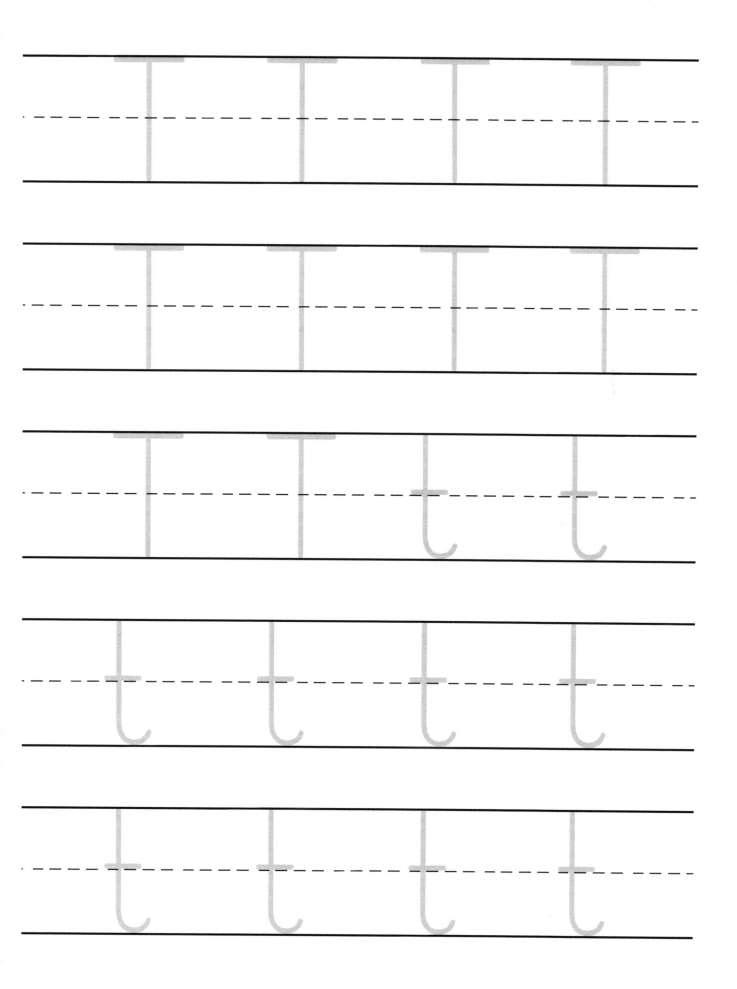

U is for

umbrella

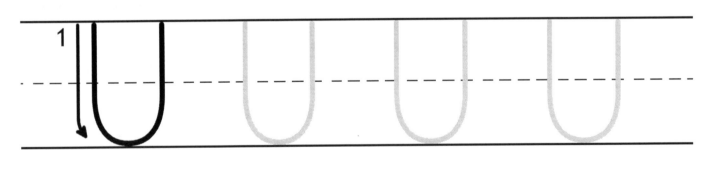

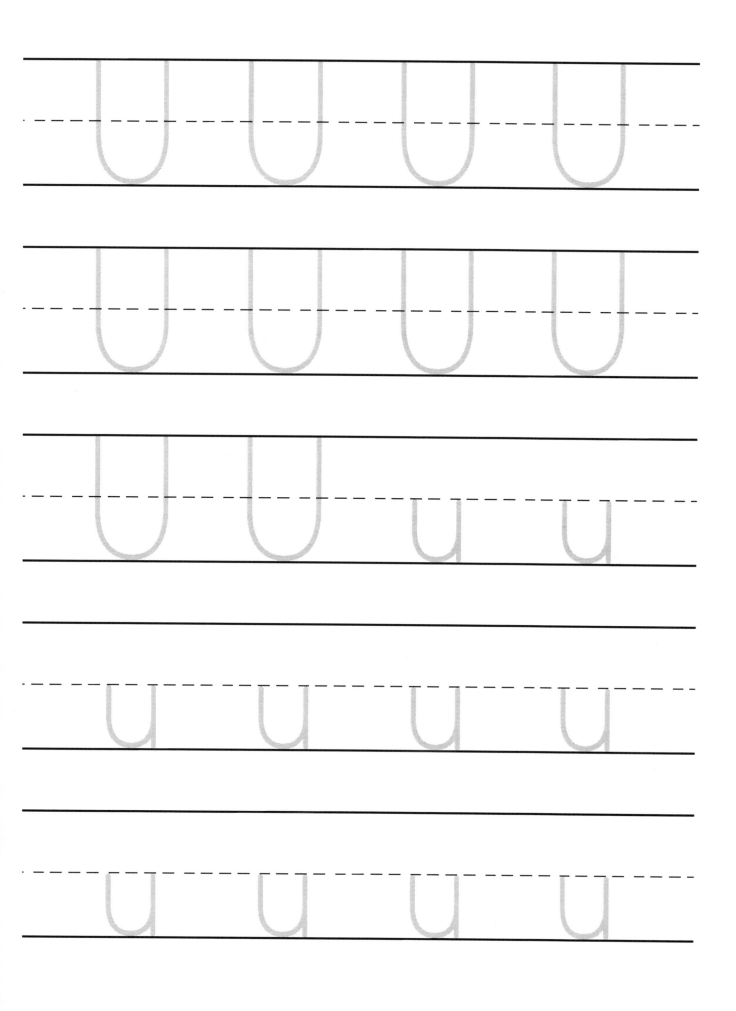

V is for

violin

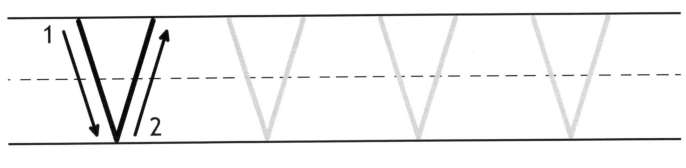

W is for

whale

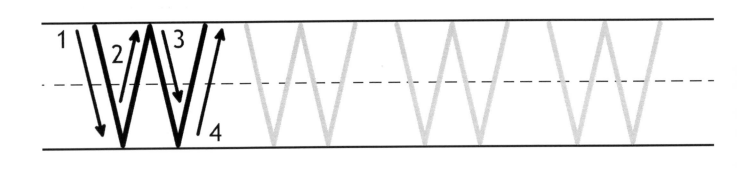

X is for

x-ray

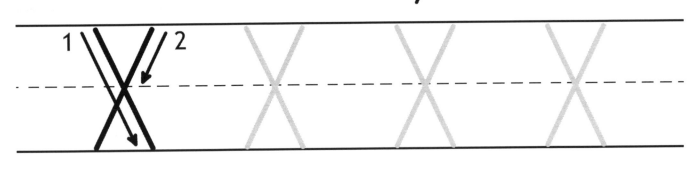

Y is for

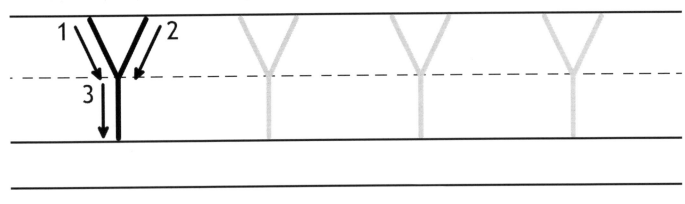

yacht

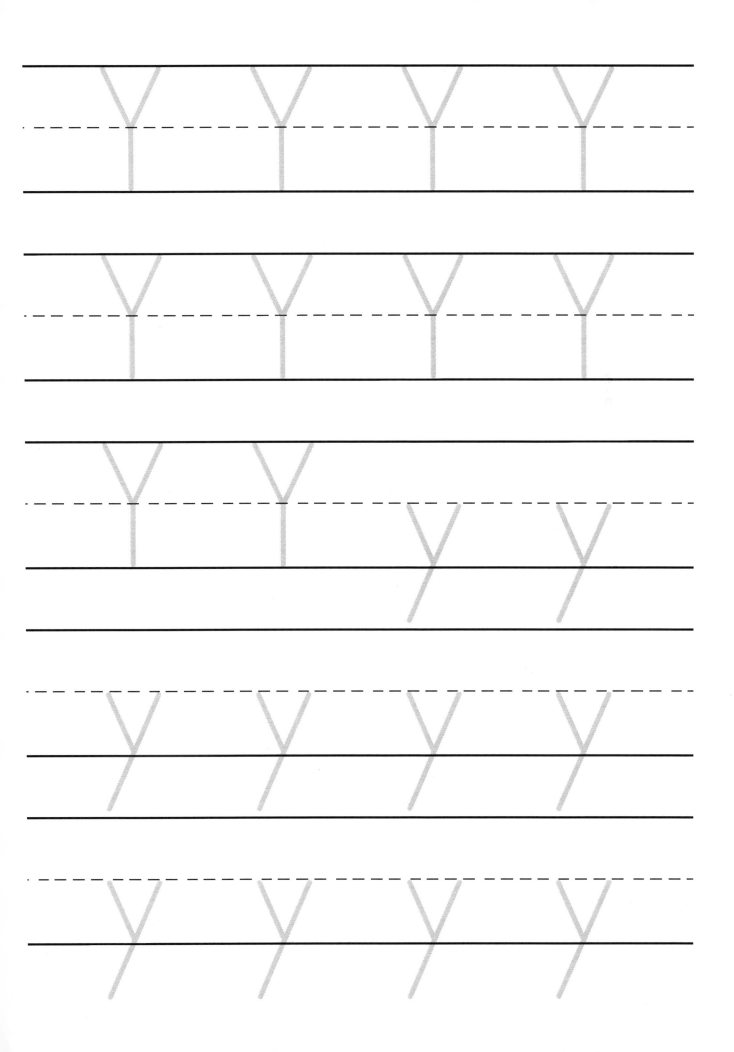

Z is for

zebra

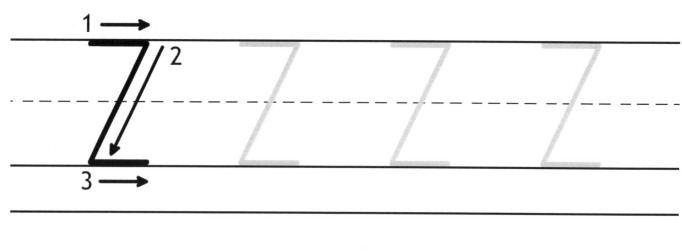

Z Z Z Z

Z Z Z Z

Z Z Z Z

Z Z Z Z

Z Z Z Z

Part 2:
Tracing words

First, follow the gray lines
to form the words.

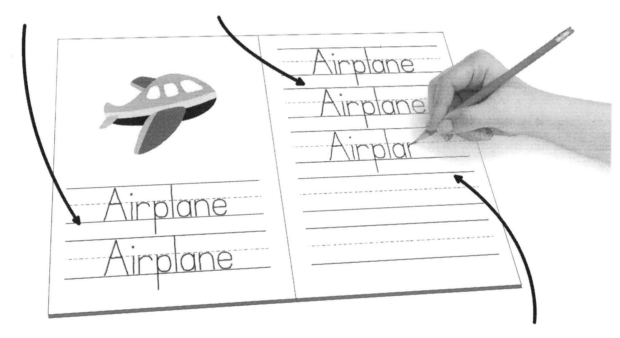

Then, try writing the words
without the gray lines.

Airplane

Airplane

Airplane

Airplane

Bicycle

Bicycle

Bicycle

Bicycle

Cake

Cake

Dinosaur

Dinosaur

Dinosaur

Dinosaur

Elephant

Elephant

Elephant

Elephant

Flower

Flower

Giraffe

Giraffe

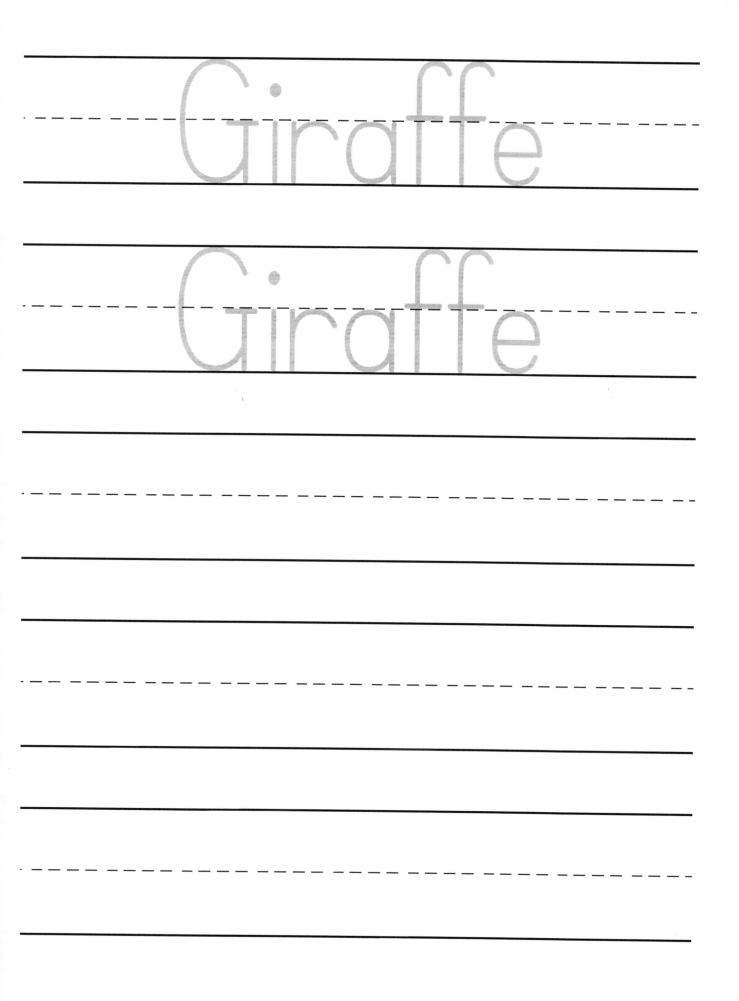

Hedgehog

Hedgehog

Hedgehog

Hedgehog

Ice-cream

Ice-cream

Ice-cream

Ice-cream

Jacket

Jacket

Jacket

Jacket

Kangaroo

Kangaroo

Kangaroo

Kangaroo

Lion

Lion

Mushroom

Mushroom

Mushroom

Mushroom

Needle

Needle

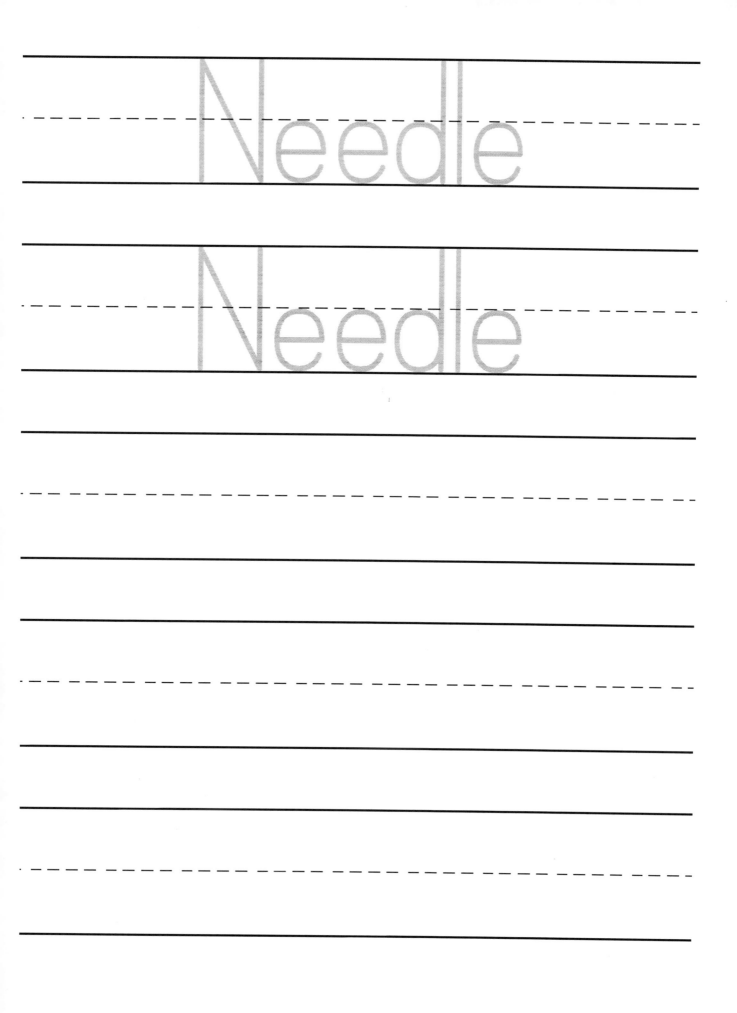

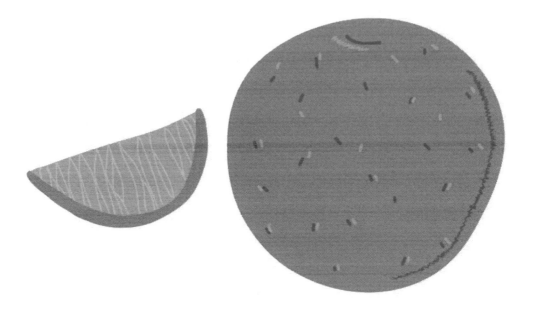

Orange

Orange

Orange

Orange

Pineapple

Pineapple

Pineapple

Pineapple

Queen

Queen

Rainbow

Rainbow

Rainbow

Rainbow

Scissors

Scissors

Scissors

Scissors

Tortoise

Tortoise

Tortoise

Tortoise

Umbrella

Umbrella

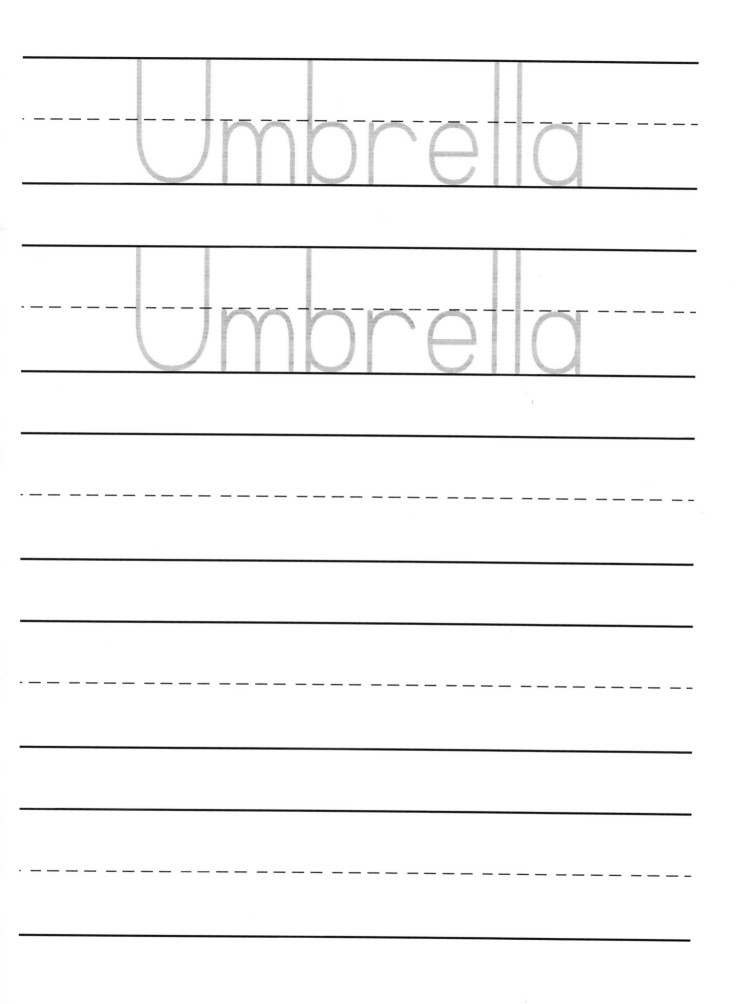

Violin

Violin

Whale

Whale

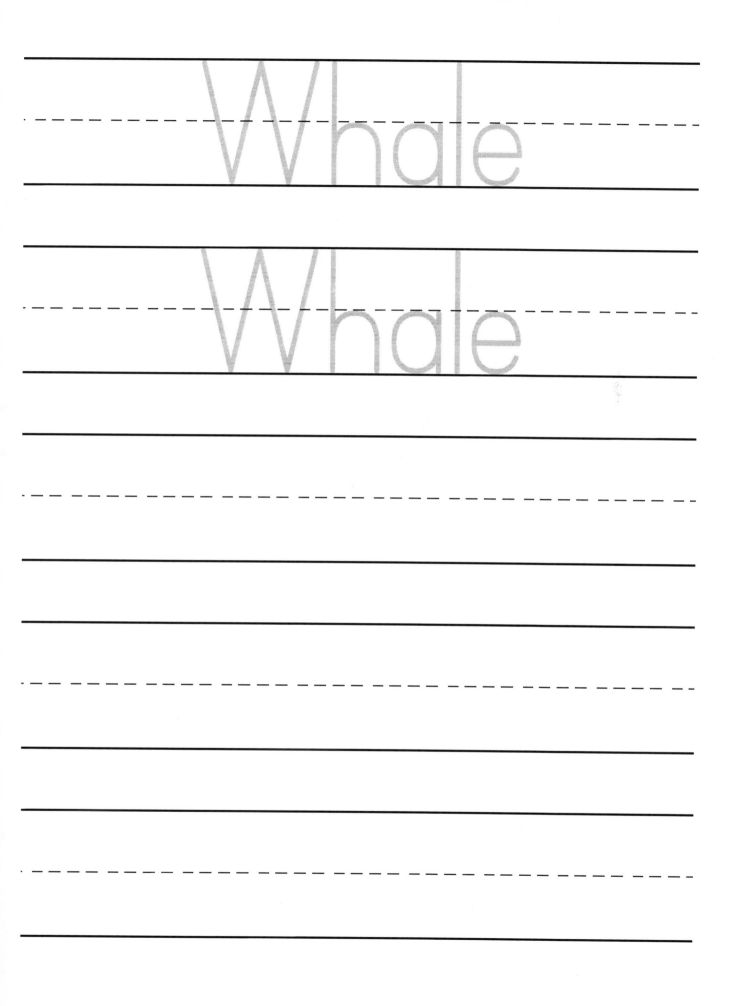

X-ray

X-ray

X-ray

X-ray

Yacht

Yacht

Yacht

Yacht

Zebra

Zebra

Zebra

Zebra

40807280R00064

Made in the USA
Middletown, DE
24 February 2017